CORE LIBRARY OF US STATES

WEST Virginia

BY EMMA HUDDLESTON

CONTENT CONSULTANT
Billy Joe Peyton, PhD
Professor of History
Department of Social & Behavioral Sciences
West Virginia State University

Core Library
An Imprint of Abdo Publishing
abdobooks.com

abdobooks.com

Published by Abdo Publishing, a division of ABDO, PO Box 398166, Minneapolis, Minnesota 55439.

Printed in the United States of America, North Mankato, Minnesota.
052022
092022

THIS BOOK CONTAINS RECYCLED MATERIALS

Cover Photo: Shutterstock Images
Interior Photos: Jon Bilous/Shutterstock Images, 4–5, 20–21, 40; Red Line Editorial, 9 (West Virginia), 9 (USA); Sean Pavone/Shutterstock Images, 10–11, 32, 45; Shutterstock Images, 12, 16 (flag), 16 (flower), 26, 43; Nature's Moments UK/Shutterstock Images, 16 (bear); Bonnie Taylor Barry/ Shutterstock Images, 16 (bird); Nancy Kennedy/Shutterstock Images, 16 (tree); Andriy Blokhin/ Shutterstock Images, 24; Everett Collection/Shutterstock Images, 28–29; Michael Dwyer/AP/ Shutterstock Images, 34–35; Breck P. Kent/Shutterstock Images, 39

Editor: Marie Pearson
Series Designer: Joshua Olson

Library of Congress Control Number: 2021951567

Publisher's Cataloging-in-Publication Data

Names: Huddleston, Emma, author.
Title: West Virginia / by Emma Huddleston
Description: Minneapolis, Minnesota : Abdo Publishing, 2023 | Series: Core library of US states | Includes online resources and index.
Identifiers: ISBN 9781532197918 (lib. bdg.) | ISBN 9781098270674 (ebook)
Subjects: LCSH: U.S. states--Juvenile literature. | Southeastern States--Juvenile literature. | West Virginia--History--Juvenile literature. | Physical geography--United States--Juvenile literature.
Classification: DDC 975.4--dc23

Population demographics broken down by race and ethnicity come from the 2019 census estimate. Population totals come from the 2020 census.

CONTENTS

CHAPTER ONE

THE MOUNTAIN STATE

A woman hikes uphill. Spruce needles crunch underfoot. She looks up. Snow dusts the top of Spruce Knob in West Virginia. It is the highest peak in the state. West Virginia lives up to its nickname, the Mountain State. The Allegheny Mountains rise up on the east side of the state. This string of mountains is part of the Appalachian Mountains, which span from Maine to Georgia.

Reaching the top of the peak, the woman looks out over the forest. She cannot see it

Hikers can catch beautiful views from Spruce Knob.

from here, but Seneca Rocks lies to the northeast. This rock cliff is popular with rock climbers. The formation is far east from the capital city, Charleston, which is located on the western side of the state. It's the largest city.

SENECA ROCKS LANDMARK

Seneca Rocks is one of the most popular tourist locations in West Virginia. The Seneca Rocks formation is located in the Monongahela National Forest. The rock structure looms 900 feet (275 m) over the North Fork River. The formation is made of a hard sandstone rock called quartzite. The rocks have a whitish-gray color. Visitors to the park can enjoy hiking, rock climbing, and exploring underground caverns.

MOUNTAINS AND VALLEYS

West Virginia is part of the Southeast. This region of the United States is typically known for agriculture and warm weather. But West Virginia is not known for either of those things. Its mountainous geography makes farming difficult in some areas. Additionally, the high elevations tend to have cool temperatures. West Virginia is the northernmost of the southeastern states. So it actually shares similarities with states in the northeastern region. These states are known for mountain ranges, snowy winters, and historic sites.

There are many small towns throughout West Virginia. The state is one of the most rural in the country. More than half the population lives in towns with fewer than 2,500 people. The towns tend to be located on ridgetops or in valleys. These areas are easiest to clear for buildings and transportation.

The Appalachian Mountains have rugged terrain. The mountains can make it hard for people to travel to jobs. So there is a lot of poverty in the state. The US government created a program to help develop the region. The program gives money to states to help build roads. It also works to create more job opportunities.

West Virginia's rural landscape benefits some businesses and organizations. For example, the National Radio Astronomy Observatory, now called the Green

Bank Observatory, studies stars and radio waves coming from outer space. It needed a quiet location with open skies. Busy cities with bright lights and radio signals could interfere with research. In 2021 the observatory's telescope began receiving updates from the NASA rover Perseverance as the rover made its landing on Mars. The observatory sent these on to NASA. The observatory was one of many organizations that found a good home in West Virginia.

PERSPECTIVES

FROM BIG CITY TO SMALL TOWN

Cathy Deobler once made her home in Los Angeles (LA), California. Now she lives in Belle, West Virginia. Deobler dreamed of running a theater. But there was intense competition in California. And rent for her apartment was pricey. So Deobler took a chance. She moved to Belle in 2018 and opened BlackRoot Theatre. Two years later, she said, "Now, I own a home and pay a third of what I paid . . . in rent for a one-bedroom apartment in LA. . . . The kindness and generosity of the people here have transformed this valley girl into a Mountaineer."

MAP OF WEST VIRGINIA

West Virginia is part of the Southeast. But it shares many similarities with states in the Northeast region. How does this map help you understand West Virginia?

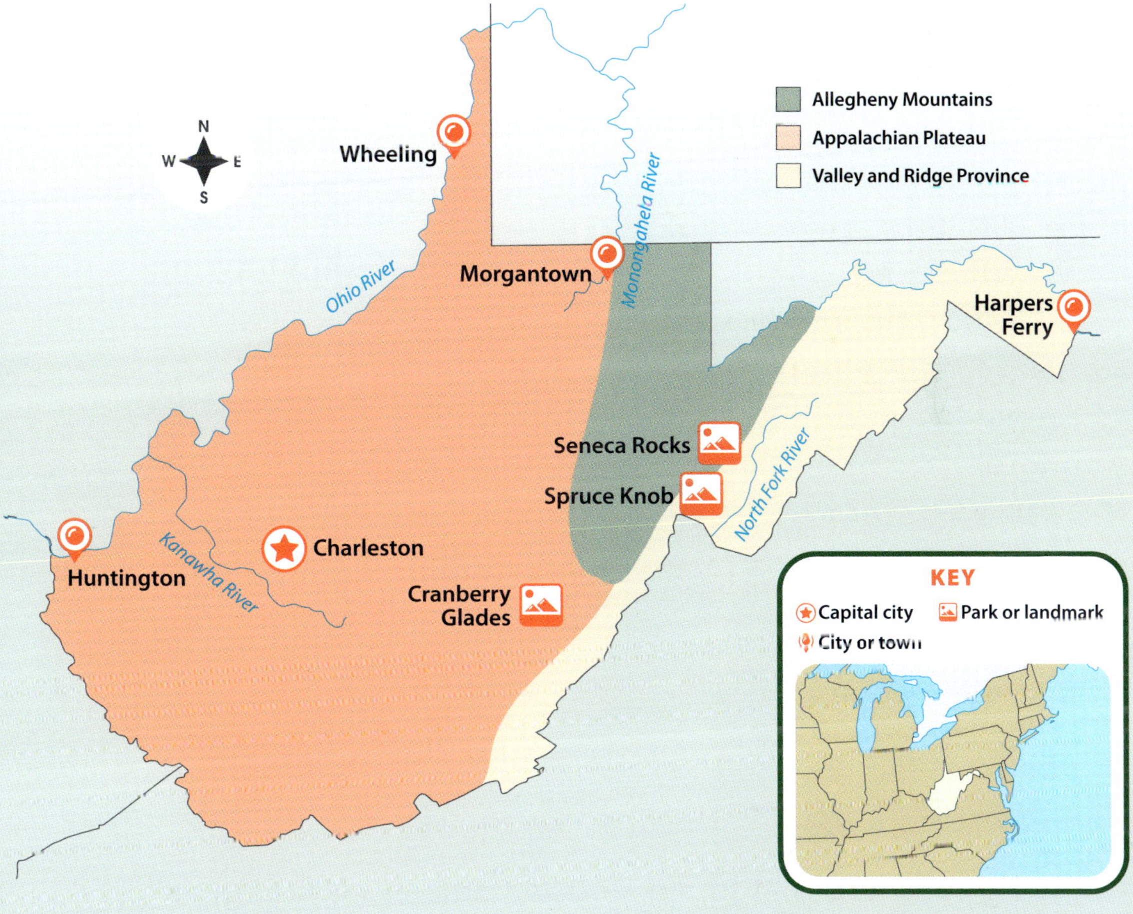

CHAPTER TWO

HISTORY OF WEST VIRGINIA

Hunters came to the West Virginia area 14,000 years ago. They were searching for mammoths. Many settled in the Ohio and Kanawha River valleys. In 9000 BCE, approximately 11,000 years ago, people living there hunted smaller animals. They also fished and gathered plants for food.

From 500 BCE to 100 CE, the Adena lived in the Kanawha Valley. They built round houses from wood and bark. They made stone tools including axes, arrowheads, and spears.

The Kanawha River was an important source of food for ancient peoples living near it.

Grave Creek Mound is in Moundsville, West Virginia.

The Adena were also called Mound Builders. They built earth and stone mounds. Earth mounds were for burying their dead. Some Adena mounds are still visible in the state today.

Eventually the Adena gave way to the Fort Ancient culture. This culture had larger villages with more families living there. They farmed corn, beans, and squash. They ate clams and mussels caught in rivers.

MORE PEOPLE ARRIVE

Fort Ancient people were pushed off their land by Haudenosaunee (Iroquois) nations in the 1600s.

The Haudenosaunee peoples came from what are now New York and other eastern states. European settlers had forced the Haudenosaunee to move from their lands. So the Haudenosaunee overtook Fort Ancient villages. They hunted in the area. More American Indians came to West Virginia from other regions. These included Cherokee, Shawnee, and Lenape nations. The Cherokee came from southeastern regions. They lived in the Appalachian Mountains in the east. They grew crops and hunted bears and deer. They used stone knives and axes.

Also during the 1600s, French and English explorers came to West Virginia. French people traded with American Indians. The French bought furs from them. In exchange, American Indians got guns and other tools. But English settlers wanted control of the land. The Lenape, Shawnee, and nations of the Haudenosaunee Confederacy signed treaties with the English. But the English and the American Indians had different understandings of these treaties. The English understood the treaties to give them control of the land in this region. For American Indians in the area, land was something to be shared. It did not belong to individual people.

When war broke out between the French and English settlers, many American Indian nations sided with the French. American Indians fought to protect their lands from the English. But the French lost the war against the English. The English took control of even more land as a result. English settlers continued to move into American Indian territories. Relations were tense. And English settlement brought diseases that killed many American Indians. By 1768 most American Indian nations in the area had signed treaties giving up their lands. They moved west.

BECOMING A STATE

West Virginia was originally part of the state of Virginia. During the American Civil War (1861–1865), Southern states including Virginia seceded from the Union to form the Confederacy. Southern slaveholders wanted to continue slavery. But other Americans wanted slavery to become illegal. Leaders in western Virginia wanted to stay in the Union. They disagreed with the other Virginia leaders. So they met in Wheeling in 1861. They voted to become a separate territory from Virginia. They stayed with the Union. On June 20, 1863, West Virginia became the thirty-fifth US state.

HARPERS FERRY RAID

John Brown wanted to end slavery. In 1859 Brown and a small group of followers organized a raid of Harpers Ferry in what is now West Virginia. This location had a supply of weapons. Brown believed he could give the weapons to local enslaved people, who would then join the raid and overthrow the slaveholders. But most did not join. Seventeen people were killed during the raid, including several Black people. Brown and his surviving followers were caught and sentenced to death. The raid on Harpers Ferry brought the United States one step closer to the Civil War. It showed people were willing to kill and die for their stances on slavery.

WEST VIRGINIA
QUICK FACTS

Each US state has its own unique history and culture. How do these state facts and symbols help you better understand West Virginia?

Abbreviation: WV
Nickname: The Mountain State
Motto: *Montani semper liberi* (Mountaineers are always free)
Date of Statehood: June 20, 1863
Capital: Charleston
Population: 1,793,716
Area: 24,230 square miles (62,755 sq km)

STATE SYMBOLS

State animal
Black bear

State flower
Rhododendron

State bird
Northern cardinal

State tree
Sugar maple

West Virginia's population grew after the war. Jobs drew people to the state. Formerly enslaved Black people moved from southern states. European families came from Europe or other US states. Many worked in coal mining and on railroads. Others worked in the steel and logging industries. In 1965 the US government built highways. The roads connected small towns. Near the Ohio River, Wheeling and Huntington grew. The river and surrounding land provided water and space for building. For similar reasons, other businesses and cities grew in the Kanawha, Monongahela, and Ohio valleys.

GOVERNMENT AND MODERN LIFE

West Virginia's state government has three branches. The legislative branch creates and passes bills, which are ideas for laws. It's made of two groups. The Senate has 34 members. The House of Delegates has 100 members. The governor leads the executive branch. This branch signs bills into law. The judicial branch is the court system. It interprets the law and applies it to court cases.

PERSPECTIVES

FEDERAL RECOGNITION FOR AMERICAN INDIAN PEOPLES

Federal recognition allows American Indian peoples to operate their own governments. They can also get funding from the US government, often for housing, health, and education. Many American Indian communities struggle in these areas as a result of previous actions by the US government. But it is not easy for American Indian peoples to get federal recognition. For example, tribes must prove that they have had a tribal political system that is separate from the US government. The tribe's political system must have existed prior to 1900. This can be difficult and expensive to prove.

No American Indian nations in West Virginia are recognized by the federal government. The state government does not recognize any tribes either. But some American Indians, including Cherokee people, live in the state. There are several complex reasons for the lack of recognition. However, American Indians in the state continue to work toward being recognized.

STRAIGHT TO THE SOURCE

Historian David R. Zimring wrote about the challenges people in the western part of Virginia faced when they tried to become their own state. The US Constitution says that a state forming out of an existing state needs the original state's permission. Virginia would not be able to grant that permission until after the war. But people in the west did not believe Virginia would allow it:

> *Supporters of the new state responded to their opponents by arguing that waiting until after the end of the war meant disaster for western Virginia. . . . If the Union defeated the Confederacy and brought Virginia back into the Union intact, the east would seize control of the state again.*

Source: David R. Zimring. "Secession in Favor of the Constitution." *West Virginia History*, vol. 3, no. 2 (Fall 2009), p. 33, jstor.org. Accessed 18 Jan. 2021.

CONSIDER YOUR AUDIENCE

Read this passage closely. Adapt it for a different audience, such as your younger friends. Write a blog post conveying this same information to the new audience. Write it so it can be understood by them. How does your new approach differ from the original, and why?

CHAPTER THREE

GEOGRAPHY AND CLIMATE

West Virginia has two main geographic regions. One is the Valley and Ridge Province, which contains the Allegheny Mountains. They rise up on the eastern side of the state. The mountains get the most rainfall. Rain drains to lower lands. It helps fill the state's many rivers. The soil in the mountains is rocky and thin. Crops do not grow well there. But the valleys can be good for farming.

Valleys in the Allegheny Mountains get rainwater, which is good for farming.

The soil with limestone is good for growing fruits and raising livestock.

HOW MOUNTAINS FORM

Mountains form by plate tectonics. Earth's crust is divided into massive sections called plates. Plate tectonics describes how the plates move over time. Hundreds of millions of years ago, the plates below modern-day North America crashed into each other. For many years, the plates pushed together. Eventually they pushed upward and rose high above the ground. This formed tall mountains. Over the next 200 million years, weather shaped the mountains. Wind and water eroded the peaks. They became the Appalachian Mountains of today.

The other region is the Appalachian Plateau. This high, semi-flat land covers most of the state. The mountains are not as high here. The region contains a maze of streams, hills, and valleys. Floodplains exist near rivers and streams. Water and nutrients in the soil make it very fertile. Clay can be taken from some of the soil to make pottery.

Both regions experience four seasons. Summers are warm and humid. Winters are cold and snowy. Temperatures change depending on location. High mountain areas tend to be colder.

On average West Virginia is 1,500 feet (460 m) in elevation. This makes West Virginia the highest state east of the Mississippi River. The state's lowest point is Harpers Ferry. This eastern town

PERSPECTIVES

BIRDS IN THE ALLEGHENIES

The Alleghenies are an important habitat for many birds. The golden-winged warbler lives only at elevations higher than 2,000 feet (610 m). It prefers shrub and grass habitats on the edges of forests. Likewise the Appalachian winter wren prefers high, cold forests. Peregrine falcons often nest at high elevations. A few can be found in the Alleghenies. But they are much rarer than they used to be. In 2020 researchers knew of only one nesting pair in the state. Scientists worked to raise young falcons in the area to try to increase their numbers again.

is where the Potomac and Shenandoah Rivers come together. It is also where West Virginia, Virginia, and Maryland meet.

PLANTS AND ANIMALS

Forests cover more than 75 percent of West Virginia. People cut down many trees in the 1900s for lumber. But people have planted more trees since then to regrow forests. Hardwoods grow best in the plateau. These trees include the sugar maple. It is the state tree of West Virginia. Softwoods and evergreen trees grow in the mountains. These include pine, spruce, and dogwood trees. Rhododendron shrubs also grow here. Animals such as rabbits, foxes, and deer rely on the woods for food and shelter. West Virginia's state animal is the black bear. Black bears can be found in every county throughout the state.

The Cranberry Glades are in the eastern part of the state. This area is made up of bogs that contain

Harpers Ferry is one of many small towns in West Virginia.

The brook trout lives in cold streams.

decaying plant material known as peat. These types of bogs are typically found farther north. They exist in West Virginia because the high elevation causes cold temperatures. Many unique plants grow in the Cranberry Glades. This includes insect-eating plants such as the pitcher plant.

Brook trout are the state fish of West Virginia. These fish are native to the state, and they are one of the most popular fish people try to catch. Males are known for the red color on their underbellies. Some people think brook trout are feisty and show the same Mountaineer spirit as the people living in the state.

STRAIGHT TO THE SOURCE

In December 2020, the New River Gorge National Park became the first national park in West Virginia. Senators Shelley Moore Capito and Joe Manchin led the efforts to establish the national park. In a statement, they wrote:

> *The New River National Gorge will be treasured and enjoyed for generations to come.*
>
> *As West Virginians, we all know that the New River Gorge is perhaps the best-known landmark in West Virginia because of its breathtaking natural beauty and elements of unique Appalachian history and culture. Now, the rest of the nation—and world—can know it too.*

Source: Shelley Moore Capito and Joe Manchin. "Sharing Wild and Wonderful with the World." *Register-Herald*, 22 Dec. 2020, register-herald.com. Accessed 21 Jan. 2021.

WHAT'S THE BIG IDEA?

Take a close look at this passage. What is the main connection the senators make between the New River Gorge National Park and West Virginian culture? What do you think this new national park means to the state?

CHAPTER FOUR

RESOURCES AND ECONOMY

After the Civil War, West Virginia's economy depended on natural resources. Coal, oil, and gas production increased. The state relied on coal mining for much of the 1900s. By the mid-1900s, mining technology and machines replaced some human workers. People began leaving the state in search of jobs. People were still moving out of West Virginia in the 1970s. The state set out to create more jobs for people living there. West Virginia created jobs

Some children worked as coal miners in the early 1900s in West Virginia. Working conditions were dangerous.

COAL MINING INDUSTRY

West Virginia's economy depends in part on coal mining. The total number of mines in the state was 126 in 2018. About half were underground mines, and half were surface mines. More than 50,000 people worked in the coal mining industry. West Virginia's mining made up 13 percent of the country's total coal production in 2018.

in chemicals, energy, automobile and aircraft manufacturing, and other industries. But it remained primarily a rural state. West Virginia's rugged land created challenges for construction.

West Virginia has many natural resources. Coal mining is the largest part of the economy. Coal is found in nearly every part of the state, especially mountainous regions. Most of the state's electricity comes from coal. In the early 2000s, West Virginia produced nearly half of the country's coal exports. Natural gas and oil are also found in the state.

However, mining can harm the environment and contribute to climate change. Climate change describes long-term changes in climate, such as warming temperatures and new patterns of rainfall. Burning fossil fuels such as coal, oil, and gas is a known cause of climate change. For these reasons, some people want to decrease the use of coal. They want to rely more on renewable energy, such as wind or solar energy. This shift away from coal will be a challenge for West Virginia. However, a report released in 2020 said

PERSPECTIVES

RENEWABLE ENERGY

Evan Hansen is a member of the West Virginia legislature. He wants the state government to focus on renewable energy. In 2018 more than 300 people in the state worked in the solar power business. Hansen wants those numbers to rise. Renewable energy is better for the environment. It produces less greenhouse gases than fossil fuel energy. It also creates jobs. Hansen said in 2019, "I think we're starting from scratch as far as having a conversation about change in West Virginia . . . and also the beginning of a conversation of what we can do to take advantage of these job opportunities coming along related to renewables."

Charleston is home to West Virginia's capitol building.

that getting energy from wind and solar power would actually be better for the economy of West Virginia than continuing to use coal.

OTHER INDUSTRIES

The next leading industries are chemical, steel, and wood products. Salt is found in West Virginia landforms. It is useful for making chemical products. Sand, clay, and limestone are useful for making glass, tile, and brick building materials. Companies in the state often make glass products for science labs or household appliances. Agriculture is limited by West Virginia's rugged land and thin soils. But lumber is plentiful. Monongahela National Forest is one of the largest hardwood forests in the eastern United States.

To help grow the economy, the state has increased service jobs. These jobs include government and transportation work. Phone and internet companies moved to West Virginia from larger, crowded areas. It is cheaper to run a business there than in urban areas such as Washington, DC. West Virginia is also trying to bring in more visitors to its historic sites and state parks.

EXPLORE ONLINE

Chapter Four discusses West Virginia's economy and fossil fuels such as coal. As you know, every source is different. What information does the article at the website below give about coal? How is the information from the website the same as the information in Chapter Four? What new information did you learn from the website?

THE STORY OF FOSSIL FUELS, PART 1: COAL

abdocorelibrary.com/west-virginia

Patriots
81

CHAPTER FIVE

PEOPLE AND PLACES

West Virginia may be a small state, but many famous people have come from it. Football player Randy Moss was born in Rand. Moss played in the NFL from 1998 through 2010, and then again in 2012. He was entered into the Pro Football Hall of Fame in 2018. Country music singer Brad Paisley was born in Glen Dale. Basketball player Jerry West grew up in Chelyan. In 1956 he was the first high school basketball player in the state to score

Randy Moss became one of the greatest NFL wide receivers in history.

900 points in a season. He went on to be a star at West Virginia University. Then he played professionally for the National Basketball Association with the Los Angeles Lakers. He later coached for the team.

LIVING IN WEST VIRGINIA

Living in small towns has benefits and drawbacks. Small towns sometimes lack resources. Grafton has a shortage of teachers. Coal mining towns may not have enough jobs for everyone. So people move or get by. Many people like the close-knit communities of small towns. Life is lived at a slower pace than in the city. There is less traffic, cleaner air, and generally less crime. Some small towns are also great for tourism. For example, Lewisburg encourages visitors to experience the works of its many local artists.

West Virginia's population mostly lives in small towns. Towns are often located near rivers and along transportation routes. Some people can get to jobs in cities. But sometimes mountains make that difficult. Sixteen percent of people live in poverty. That is higher than the national average of 10.5 percent.

White people make up the majority of West Virginia's population. Black and Latino are the next largest populations. Cherokee, Shawnee, Saponi, and Delaware people are among the American Indians living in West Virginia.

European influences are seen throughout the state. Clarksburg has an Italian Heritage Festival. More than

PERSPECTIVES

HUNGRY FOR HISTORY

Wayne Appleton, also known as Chief Grey Owl, is interested in uncovering American Indian history in West Virginia. He has Cherokee and Mohawk roots. Today Appleton is part of the Appalachian American Indians of West Virginia. This group tries to help people connect with their family histories. It works with people of many ancestries, including Cherokee or Mohawk. Appleton said, "You try to help people make contact with their history, with their heritage, and you try to help them fill in the gaps. They're hungry for their history."

100,000 people attend the weekend event. They eat traditional foods such as pasta and fritti, or fried dough. They play games. American Indian influences are also seen, particularly in city and landform names. For example, the name of the Monongahela River means "river with sliding banks" in the Seneca language.

PLACES

Large cities such as Charleston and Huntington are home to colleges. West Virginia University is in Morgantown. Even those not attending the university can enjoy its music, theater, and dance productions. Several theaters and museums are also located in these cities. Charleston hosts Live on the Levee in the summer. Crowds sit in an outdoor theater facing the Kanawha River. Musicians and other entertainers perform in the theater.

Many historic sites are located in West Virginia. Independence Hall in Wheeling is called the birthplace of the state. It is where important meetings happened

At Cass Scenic Railroad State Park, visitors can learn about historic logging practices and ride a steam logging train.

to separate West Virginia from Virginia. In Huntington, a museum operates a recreated village from the 1800s. Visitors can enter a log church and a blacksmith shop. These buildings are set up to show visitors what it was like to live in West Virginia many years ago.

People can enjoy beautiful views at Hawks Nest State Park.

Beyond historic sites, people enjoy outdoor activities. West Virginia is home to more than 30 state parks. People camp and fish. They can ride horses or go white water rafting. In the winter, skiing is popular. Some parks have unique places to stay. In Seneca State Forest, a tall fire tower was made into a cabin. Visitors can see out over the trees on every side. West Virginia's mountains and valleys offer many scenic places. Cities, small towns, and many state parks offer something for everyone.

FURTHER EVIDENCE

Chapter Five discusses state parks, including Seneca State Forest. Identify one of the chapter's main points. What evidence does the author provide to support this point? The website at the link below also discusses Seneca State Forest. Find a quote on this website that supports the main point you identified. Does the quote support an existing piece of evidence in the chapter? Or does it offer a new piece of evidence?

SENECA STATE FOREST

abdocorelibrary.com/west-virginia

IMPORTANT DATES

14,000 years ago
Hunters come to the West Virginia area searching for mammoths. They settle near rivers.

500 BCE–100 CE
The Adena live in the Kanawha Valley. They make stone tools including axes, arrowheads, and spears.

1600s
Europeans force Haudenosaunee peoples from the East to what is now West Virginia. The Haudenosaunee push Fort Ancient peoples off the land. French and English explorers start coming to West Virginia.

1861
Leaders in western Virginia meet at Wheeling. They plan to separate from the state of Virginia.

1863
West Virginia becomes the thirty-fifth US state on June 20.

1900s
Coal mining is the main part of West Virginia's economy. Salt, oil, gas, and timber production are also important.

Mid-1900s
Mining technology reduces the number of human workers needed. People move out of West Virginia to look for jobs.

Early 2000s
West Virginia produces nearly half of US coal exports. Some people worry about how burning coal harms the environment.

STOP AND THINK

Tell the Tale

Chapter Two of this book discusses West Virginia's history. Imagine you are writing a blog post for students to read. Write 200 words about West Virginia's history before it became a state. How and why did West Virginia separate from Virginia to become a US state?

Dig Deeper

After reading this book, what questions do you still have about West Virginia? With an adult's help, find a few reliable sources that can help you answer your questions. Write a paragraph about what you learned.

Say What?

Studying US states and history can mean learning a lot of new vocabulary. Find five words in this book you've never heard before. Use a dictionary to find out what they mean. Then write the meanings in your own words and use each word in a new sentence.

You Are There

This book discusses West Virginia's nickname, the Mountain State. Imagine you are hiking through mountains. Write a letter home telling your friends about the experience. What plants and animals do you see? What does the climate feel like? Be sure to add plenty of detail to your notes.

GLOSSARY

agriculture
the practice of farming crops and livestock

elevation
the height above sea level

erode
to wear away by the movement of wind, water, or other natural forces

export
a good sent to another region or country for sale

federal
having to do with the national government

fertile
rich in nutrients for growing plants

habitat
the place where a plant or an animal lives

rural
having to do with the countryside

secede
to leave a political union

ONLINE RESOURCES

To learn more about West Virginia, visit our free resource websites below.

Core Library CONNECTION
FREE! COMMON CORE MULTIMEDIA RESOURCES

Visit **abdocorelibrary.com** or scan this QR code for free Common Core resources for teachers and students, including vetted activities, multimedia, and booklinks, for deeper subject comprehension.

Booklinks NONFICTION NETWORK
FREE! ONLINE NONFICTION RESOURCES

Visit **abdobooklinks.com** or scan this QR code for free additional online weblinks for further learning. These links are routinely monitored and updated to provide the most current information available.

LEARN MORE

Ceravalo, Michelle. *My West Virginia*. Headline Books, 2018.

O'Brien, Cynthia. *Encyclopedia of American Indian History and Culture*. National Geographic, 2019.

INDEX

About the Author

Emma Huddleston lives in Minnesota with her husband. She enjoys writing children's books and reading mystery novels. She has been to 18 US states and hopes to visit many more!